CAREERS IN THE
BUILDING TRADES

Plumber

Careers in the Building Trades

A Growing Demand

 Apprenticeships

 Carpenter

 Construction & Building Inspector

 Electrician

 Flooring Installer

 Heating and Cooling Technician

Masonry Worker

 Plumber

 Roofer

Working in Green Construction

CAREERS IN THE
BUILDING TRADES

A GROWING DEMAND

Plumber

Andrew Morkes

MASON CREST

Mason Crest
450 Parkway Drive, Suite D
Broomall, Pennsylvania 19008
(866) MCP-BOOK (toll-free)
www.masoncrest.com

First printing

9 8 7 6 5 4 3 2 1
ISBN (hardback) 978-1-4222-4118-9

ISBN (series) 978-1-4222-4110-3

ISBN (ebook) 978-1-4222-7688-4

Cataloging-in-Publication Data on file with the Library of Congress

Developed and Produced by National Highlights Inc.
Proofreader: Mika Jin
Interior and cover design: Yolanda Van Cooten
Production: Michelle Luke

CONTENTS

KEY ICONS TO LOOK FOR:

Words to understand: These words with their easy-to-understand definitions will increase the reader's understanding of the text while building vocabulary skills.

Sidebars: This boxed material within the main text allows readers to build knowledge, gain insights, explore possibilities, and broaden their perspectives by weaving together additional information to provide realistic and holistic perspectives.

Educational Videos: Readers can view videos by scanning our QR codes, providing them with additional educational content to supplement the text. Examples include news coverage, moments in history, speeches, iconic sports moments and much more!

Text-dependent questions: These questions send the reader back to the text for more careful attention to the evidence presented there.

Research projects: Readers are pointed toward areas of further inquiry connected to each chapter. Suggestions are provided for projects that encourage deeper research and analysis.

Series glossary of key terms: This back-of-the-book glossary contains terminology used throughout this series. Words found here increase the reader's ability to read and comprehend higher-level books and articles in this field.

INTRODUCTION

The Trades: Great Careers, Good Money, and Other Rewards

Trades workers play a major role in the success of economies throughout the world. They build structures ranging from houses to skyscrapers, keep the power on, and install and repair pipes that carry water, fuel, and other liquids to, from, and within businesses, factories, and homes, among many other job duties. Yet despite their pivotal role in our society, only 6 percent of students consider a career in the trades, according to ExploretheTrades.org. Why? Because many young people have misconceptions about the trades. They have been told that the trades are low paying, lack job security, and other untruths. In fact, working in the trades is one of the best career choices you can make. The following paragraphs provide more information on why a career in the trades is a good idea.

Good pay. Contrary to public perception, skilled trades workers earn salaries that place them firmly in the middle class. For example, average yearly salaries for plumbers, pipefitters, and steamfitters in the United States are $56,030, according to the U.S. Department of Labor. This salary is higher than the average earnings for some careers that require a bachelor's or graduate degree—including archivists ($54,570), event planners ($52,020), social workers ($50,710), recreational therapists ($48,190), and mental health counselors ($46,050). Trades workers who become managers or who launch their own businesses can have earnings that range from $90,000 to $200,000.

Strong employment prospects. There are shortages of trades workers throughout the world, according to the human resource consulting firm ManpowerGroup. In fact, trades workers are the most in-demand occupational field in the Americas, Europe, the Middle East, and Africa. They ranked fourth in the Asia-Pacific region. Plumbers are in especially strong demand in the United States, Canada, Norway, Germany, Switzerland, Russia, and Australia.

Provides a comfortable life without a bachelor's or graduate degree. For decades in the United States and other countries, there has been an emphasis on earning a college degree as the key to life success. But studies show that only 35 percent of future jobs in the U.S. will require a four-year degree or higher. With college tuition continuing to increase and the chances of landing a good job out of college decreasing, a growing number of people are entering apprenticeship programs to prepare for careers in the trades. And unlike college students, apprentices receive a salary while learning, and they don't have to pay off loans after they complete their education. It's a good feeling to start your career without $50,000 to $200,000 in college loans.

Rewarding work environment and many career options. A career in the trades is fulfilling because you get to use both your hands and your head to solve problems and make the world a better place. You can work at a construction site, at a manufacturing plant, at a business, and in other settings. Many trades workers launch their own businesses.

Jobs can't be offshored. Trades careers involve hands-on work that requires the worker to be on-site to do his or her job. As a result, there is no chance that your position will be offshored to a foreign country. In an uncertain employment atmosphere, that's encouraging news.

Job opportunities are available throughout the United States and the world. There is a need for trades workers in small towns and big cities. If demand for their skills is not strong in their area, they can move to other cities, states, or countries where demand is higher.

Are the Trades Right for Me?

Test your interest in the trades. How many of these statements do you agree with?

- [ ] My favorite class in school is shop.

- [ ] I like doing household repairs.

- [ ] I like to use power and hand tools.

- [ ] I like projects that allow me to work with my hands.

- [ ] I enjoy observing work at construction sites.

- [ ] I like to build and fix things.

- [ ] I like to watch home-repair shows on TV and the internet.

- [ ] I don't mind getting my hands dirty.

- [ ] I like solving problems.

- [ ] I am good at math.

- [ ] I like to figure out how things work.

If many of the statements above describe you, then you should consider a career in the trades. But you don't need to select a career right now. Check out this book on a career as a plumber and other books in the series to learn more about occupational paths in the trades. Good luck with your career exploration!

Words to Understand

blueprints: A reproduction of a technical plan for the construction of a home or other structure. Blueprints are created by licensed architects.

carbon footprint: The amount of greenhouse gas (carbon dioxide, methane, ozone, etc.) emissions created by a person, product, organization, or event. Greenhouse gases warm the earth's atmosphere.

self-employed: Working for oneself as a small business owner, rather than for a corporation or other employer. Self-employed people must generate their own income and provide their own fringe benefits (such as health insurance).

sprinkler system: A fire protection system that shoots out water when high heat from a fire is detected.

water softener: A device that removes hard minerals such as calcium and magnesium from water. Hard water can cause a scaly buildup on pipes, heating elements in appliances, dishes, and even our skin.

CHAPTER 1

What Do Plumbers Do?

Imagine what life would be like if you couldn't turn on the kitchen tap and get a drink of refreshing water, take a shower or bath, or even flush the toilet. In short, life would be much harder and dirtier. Plumbers are the skilled-trades workers who install and repair pipes that carry liquids or gases to, from, and within our homes, businesses, and factories. They also work at construction sites and on big infrastructure projects such as highways, bridges, and pipelines. Plumbers are some of the most in-demand workers in the trades.

Some plumbers operate their own businesses. Others work for construction companies and contractors. To learn their skills and obtain experience, aspiring plumbers complete four- to five-year apprenticeships or training programs at technical schools. Others receive informal training from experienced plumbers, through the military, or at contractor schools.

■ *A plumber at a factory troubleshoots a malfunctioning pipe.*

U.S. News & World Report recently ranked the career of plumber as the third-best construction job, and this occupation typically ranks high in other "best job" lists. This is a good career for those who like to work with their hands, who don't mind getting dirty (really dirty, at times!), who like solving problems, and want the opportunity to make a good living without earning a four-year degree.

■ *Learn more about plumbing career paths (recreation, medical, public water supply safety).*

Types of Plumbers

Your job duties as a plumber will vary depending on where you work, although a plumber who works in one sector can also work in other sectors if they have enough skill, training, and experience.

Residential plumbers are the type of plumbers that you're probably most familiar with. They come to your house when your sink gets clogged or a pipe starts leaking. They work for plumbing service companies or have their own businesses. Typical duties for residential plumbers include:

- Repairing leaky pipes
- Unclogging sewer lines
- Thawing frozen pipes
- Installing new water, drainage, and heating systems
- Cutting, bending, and joining pipes and fittings
- Providing cost estimates to customers
- Servicing gas and oil-fired central heating systems and radiators
- Installing and repairing household appliances such as water heaters, washing machines, and **water softeners**
- Handling emergency calls such as serious water leaks, burst pipes, or boiler breakdowns.

■ *Aqueducts built by the ancient Romans are marvels of plumbing engineering and construction. Above, the Roman aqueduct of Segovia, Spain, one of the best-preserved elevated Roman aqueducts.*

You'll like working as a residential plumber if you enjoy interacting with others, helping people solve problems, traveling to a new job site every day, and working on your own.

■ *A plumber discusses the rewards and challenges of the job.*

A Little History

- The ancient Egyptians were one of the first cultures to use piping to carry water in and out of buildings.
- The ancient Romans built vast aqueduct systems to transport water. The first such aqueduct was built for the city of Roma and was operational in 312 B.C. Approximately one-thousand Roman aqueducts are known today.
- The flush toilet was invented in 1596.
- In 1738, the valve-type flush toilet was invented.
- In 1775, a version of the type of toilet we use today was patented.
- In 1829, the Tremont Hotel in Boston, Massachusetts, became the first hotel to have indoor plumbing.
- The first packaged toilet paper was invented in 1857.

Sources: Roto-Rooter, Smithsonian

Commercial plumbers work on large plumbing systems at schools, hospitals, water parks, sports stadiums, and shopping centers. These buildings feature complex, industrial-grade pipes and fixtures. Thousands of people use these systems regularly. Typical duties for commercial plumbers include:

- Laying water and sewer delivery and drainage pipes by following blueprints
- Connecting these pipes to municipal water and sewage systems
- Installing and maintaining large-scale waste removal and water-supply systems
- Installing fixtures in washrooms, industrial kitchens, bar areas, and pool and recreation areas
- Installing sprinkler systems
- In some instances, installing water heaters or boilers, although these tasks are typically done by heating and cooling technicians.

Commercial plumbers who work at finished buildings perform a variety of maintenance and repair tasks, including:

- Repairing leaky pipes
- Unclogging blocked sewer lines
- Thawing frozen pipes or water mains
- Repairing any appliance or system that provides drinking water or gets rid of wastewater or sewage
- Handling emergency calls such as serious water leaks, burst pipes, or boiler breakdowns
- Clearing drains blocked by grease or installing special traps that prevent such blockages
- Ensuring that all plumbing infrastructure meets applicable health codes and regulations for commercial establishments
- Replacing old or poorly working plumbing appliances and systems.

■ *A plumbing contractor solders copper pipes at a job site.*

You'll enjoy being a commercial plumber if you like working as a member of a team, like having a wide range of job duties, and are willing to work at night and on weekends to keep projects on schedule (if you're working at a construction site). If you're employed as a maintenance plumber at a commercial building, you'll probably have more of a 9-to-5 work schedule, but you will occasionally need to cover work shifts at night and on weekends.

Green construction, or green building, is a relatively new concept that stresses water and energy efficiency, the use of eco-friendly or fewer construction materials (when possible), indoor environmental quality, and the structure's overall effects on its site or the larger community. *Green plumbers* perform job duties such as:

- Helping residential customers or commercial contractors reduce water usage, recycle water, and make use of sustainable resources via the use of water-saving technologies, solar power for hot water, and installing hybrid water heaters that provide hot water on demand, and that have a low **carbon footprint**

- Conducting water audits of homes and businesses to help reduce the amount of water being used

- Installing and servicing water-saving devices, the piping systems that attach to solar power systems, and other related hardware and systems.

Becoming a green plumber is a good career choice if you love protecting the environment, enjoy coming up with creative solutions to challenging problems, have good analytical skills, and like interacting with others.

■ *An Australian plumber discusses his career.*

■ *A pipefitter installs an underfloor heating system.*

Becoming a Boss

After three to five years on the job, skilled plumbers can be promoted to the position of *foreman*. These mid-level managers supervise a team of plumbers and apprentices, while also pitching in with the work, when necessary. Major responsibilities for foremen include:

- Creating work schedules and making sure that crews meet project deadlines
- Inspecting finished work to make sure that it meets building codes and project specifications
- Meeting with job superintendents throughout the project to ensure that the work is being completed on-budget, on-time, and meeting other project guidelines
- Assessing the work of apprentices as they do their jobs to ensure that their skills and plumbing and general construction knowledge are improving
- Ensuring that all company equipment, tools, and vehicles are in good working order
- Ordering work supplies and materials as necessary
- Maintaining a safe work environment.

You'll like working as a foreman if you enjoy managing others, taking on a considerable degree of responsibility and meeting deadlines, traveling to multiple construction sites to supervise work teams, and occasionally working at night and on weekends to meet project deadlines. A skilled foreman can advance to the position of project superintendent or owner of a construction firm.

Starting Your Own Contracting Business

About 10 percent of plumbers in the United States are **self-employed**, according to the U.S. Department of Labor. Self-employed workers are known as contractors. They perform the same tasks as commercial or residential plumbers, but they own their own businesses. A plumbing contracting firm might consist of one person or it might employ many plumbers, office staff, and other support workers. Many contractors provide services to residential customers. They thaw frozen pipes or water mains, install new toilets and sinks, fix leaky pipes, or repair boilers. A contracting firm that is hired for a commercial project might be tasked with a specific duty throughout the project—such as installing all the plumbing piping and fixtures for all the washrooms in a new sports stadium—or they may be tasked with a variety of plumbing-related responsibilities.

There are many reasons to become a plumbing contractor. Most contractors cite the fact that they get to be their own bosses and build a business as the main reasons why they like this career path. Contractors also like the fact that the work is constantly changing and that they can earn much more money than the average plumber if their business is successful.

But it's not always fun and rewarding to be a business owner. If you own a large business, you have a responsibility to provide work and pay to your employees. This means you'll have to constantly market your business at community events, in the newspaper, and on the internet and social media. You'll also have to handle office-related tasks such as appointment scheduling, invoicing (and some customers don't pay their bills), and payroll. Unless you hire office staff, these tasks will take you away from being out in the field providing services to customers. Although there are many challenges to owning a business, most contractors find this career path both personally and financially rewarding.

They Were Plumbers!?

Did you know that Michael Flatley was a plumber before he wowed the world as a dancer and choreographer of the internationally known Irish dance shows *Lord of the Dance* and *Riverdance*? He worked in his father's plumbing business while training for Ireland's world dance competition. "At the time, I was still digging ditches for dad, but my father wanted me to win the Irish crown almost as much as I did, so he gave me time off to dance in the garage," Flatley recalled in his biography, *Lord of the Dance: My Story.* Here are a few other well-known people who worked as plumbers before becoming successful in another field:

■ *The well-known actor Michael Caine once worked as a plumber.*

- Academy Award-winning-actor Michael Caine was a plumber's assistant before hitting it big as an actor.
- Joe Cocker initially worked as a plumber before becoming a Grammy-winning singer.
- Heavy-metal singer Ozzy Osbourne worked as a plumber's apprentice for a short time before he decided that he would rather stand in front of a microphone than a clogged pipe.

Sources: Chicago Sun-Times, The Telegraph, Reuters

■ *Learn more about the career of pipefitter.*

Related Career Paths

Plumbers who complete specialized education and training are qualified to work in many related fields. Here are a few popular options:

Pipefitters install high-pressure and low-pressure pipe systems that carry gases, chemicals, and acids. They usually work in commercial, manufacturing, and industrial settings. They also inspect and repair existing pipe systems, including those used to create electricity and those used in heating and cooling systems.

Pipefitters can further specialize, working as *sprinkler fitters,* who install, maintain, and repair automatic fire sprinkler systems; *gasfitters,* who install and repair pipes that provide natural gas to cooling and heating systems and to stoves, as well as pipes that transport natural gas or those that provide oxygen to patients in hospitals; and *steamfitters,* who install and repair pipe systems that move steam under high pressure.

Pipelayers install and repair pipes for sewer and drainage systems and oil and gas lines. These pipes are constructed out of iron, clay, concrete, and plastic.

Workplace Safety

Plumbers have one of the highest rates of injuries and illnesses of all careers, according to the U.S. Department of Labor. The most common injuries to plumbers include:

How to Stay Safe on the Job

Plumbers must follow strong safety practices to avoid injury. They wear protective gear such as heavy gloves, face shields, respirators, coveralls, and steel-toed work shoes with non-slip soles. Here are a few safety measures to follow if you work as a plumber:

- Be extremely careful on ladders or when working at heights or in areas with wet floors.
- Avoid being exposed to sewage by wearing gloves, rubber boots, and other protective gear.
- Wash your hands vigorously with antibacterial soap and water as often as possible, and decontaminate your equipment after use.
- Don't eat or drink on the job site—especially if you are working near sewage, chemicals, or other hazardous substances.
- Do not wear your work clothes home. Keep them separate from your regular laundry, and wash them separately.
- Use heat-insulating gloves and face/eye shields when working on hot pipes. Make sure to drain pipes of remaining water before you open them.
- Use power tools that have a ground fault circuit interrupter to avoid electrocution. Check your equipment for frayed electrical cords and other issues that might put you in danger.
- Properly ventilate all work areas. Wear a respirator (an artificial breathing device that protects a person from breathing dust, smoke, or other toxic substances) if working around hazardous materials.
- Keep work areas clear of clutter to avoid falls or other injuries.
- Address your concerns about project safety with your foreman or the job superintendent.

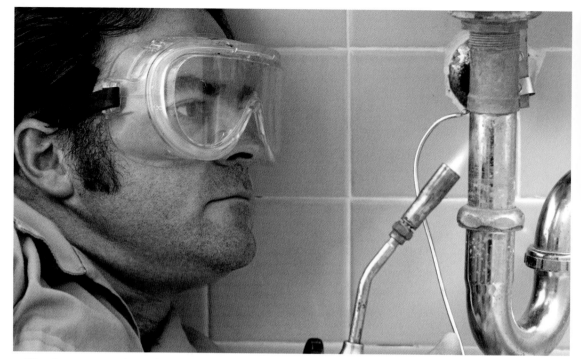

■ *Plumbers must take safety precautions—such as wearing protective eyewear—when using a welding torch to connect pipes.*

- Cuts from sharp tools

- Burns from hot pipes and soldering equipment

- Falls from ladders

- Back injury and muscle stress/strain

- Eye injuries caused by foreign objects entering the eyes during welding or soldering of pipes

- Exposure to hazardous chemicals, fumes, and substances; raw sewage; and other toxic or carcinogenic (known to cause cancer) substances

- Knee, leg, or other injuries caused by kneeling for long periods or slipping on wet or icy surfaces.

Other injuries, fatalities, and health conditions are caused by overexertion while lifting, being struck by a falling object, repetitive movements, molds and fungi, and loud noises from machinery and tools.

Text-Dependent Questions

1. What type of plumbers work on large plumbing systems at schools, hospitals, water parks, sports stadiums, and shopping centers?

2. What are some of the best aspects of a career as a plumbing contractor?

3. What kinds of safety gear do plumbers use to protect themselves?

Research Project

Talk to a plumbing contractor about what it's like to own a business. Ask if you can job shadow him or her in the office and at job sites.

CHAPTER 2

Tools of the Trade

Cutting, Bending, Extracting, Smoothing, & Measuring Tools

chisel: A hand tool with a shaped, sharp cutting edge that is used to cut, chip, or carve metal, wood, or stone.

drill: A hand or power tool that is fitted with a cutting tool attachment or driving tool attachment; it is used to cut into material ranging from metal and plastic, to wood and stone.

hacksaw: A hand saw that is used to cut through metal pipe, hardware, nuts and bolts, and screws, as well as plastic pipe.

laser measure: A device that allows users to take distance measurements instantly.

metal file: A tool that removes burrs (loose pieces of metal or plastic) and smoothes the edges of pipes after cutting. Removing burrs and smoothing the surface allows for a tight connection between pipes and fittings.

pipe cutter: A tool that can be used in place of a hacksaw to cut steel and copper pipes.

pliers: A hand tool that is used to hold objects firmly, as well as bend and compress a variety of materials. The most-popular type for plumbers is the tongue-and-groove plier, which has a slip joint feature that allows the size range of its jaws to be increased and decreased.

power saw: A cutting device that is battery- or electric-powered.

tape measure: A flexible ruler made up of fiber glass, a metal strip, cloth, or plastic.

wire brush: A tool that is used to remove burrs (metal or plastic fragments) after cutting pipe.

Clearing Tools

closet auger: A manual tool that is used to clear clogs. It is specifically designed for toilets.

hand auger: A hand-cranked tool that has a 25-foot-long (7.62 meters) flexible steel cable; it is used to clear blocked pipes. Sometimes called a **plumber's snake**.

plunger: A tool, consisting of a rubber suction cup that is attached to a stick, which is used to clear clogs and blockages in toilets, drains, and pipes.

Joining Tools

hammer: A hand tool with a metal or wooden head that is mounted to the handle at right angles; it is used to drive or remove nails or break-up old construction materials.

pipe threader: A device that is used to cut threads or grooves into the end of a metal or plastic pipe; doing so allows the pipe to be attached to a connector.

propane torch: A device that is used to heat, or sweat, copper pipes (tubing) and fittings so that they can be welded together with solder.

screwdriver: A manual or powered device that turns screws; available with a flat-tened, cross-shaped style (known as a flathead screwdriver), or with a star-shaped tip that fits into the head of a screw to turn it (often referred to as a Phillips® screw-driver).

wrench: A hand tool that is used for gripping, turning, tightening, fastening, and loos-ening items like pipes, pipe fittings, and nuts and bolts.

Computer Technology

building information modeling software: A computer application that uses a 3D model-based process that helps construction, architecture, and engineering professionals to more efficiently plan, design, build, and manage buildings and infra-structure.

drain inspection camera: A water-resistant device that can be snaked through pipes to take photos and video of clogs or other plumbing issues.

office management software: A computer application that helps users track finances and manage billing, draft correspondence, and perform other tasks.

CHAPTER 3
Terms of the Trade

backflow: When the normal flow of water or other substances into a drinking-water distribution system is reversed by an unintended source (i.e., a bad thing).

black water: Polluted water that includes solid and liquid human body waste and the water that is flushed after toilet use.

blueprints: A reproduction of a technical plan for the construction of a home or other structure. Blueprints are created by licensed architects.

building codes: A series of rules established by local, state, regional, and national governments that ensure safe construction. The National Standard Plumbing Code, which was developed by the Plumbing-Heating-Cooling Contractors Association, is an example of a building code in the United States.

burrs: Loose pieces of metal or plastic that are present after a pipe or plumbing fixture is cut. Plumbers use a metal file or sandpaper to remove the burrs and smooth the edges of pipes.

corrosion: A chemical reaction that causes deterioration of metal, stone, or other materials.

drain: A pipe that carries wastewater and sewage to municipal treatment plants.

effluent: Treated or untreated wastewater that can come from homes or treatment plants, sewers, or factories.

fire-resistant cloth: A specially treated cloth used by plumbers when soldering with an open-flame propane torch. They use the cloth to cover nearby surfaces that can easily start on fire.

fittings: Any types of hardware that are used to connect straight pipe or tubing sections, connect different shapes or sizes of pipes, regulate the flow of fluids, and for other purposes.

grease interceptor: A type of hardware that is used, typically outside a building, to catch grease before it passes into the sewage system. Grease is a common substance that clogs pipes.

grease trap: A type of grease interceptor that is installed inside a building facility to catch the grease near its source.

green construction: The planning, design, construction, and operation of structures in an environmentally responsible manner. Green construction stresses energy and water efficiency,

the use of eco-friendly construction materials (when possible), indoor environmental quality, and the structure's overall effects on its site or the larger community. Also known as green building.

greywater: Water that comes from showers, sinks, dishwashers, and washing machines that is relatively clean.

greywater recycling system: A water recovery system that re-uses greywater from showers, sinks, etc. for non-drinking purposes, such as for toilet flushing.

metal alloy: A mixture of two metals or metal and another substance.

pipe: A hollow tube of metal, plastic, or other material that carries water, oil, gas, or other substances.

plumbing fixture: A plumbing device, appliance, or another object that can be temporarily or permanently fixed in place. Water or wastewater moves through these fixtures.

polyvinyl chloride pipes: Lightweight, durable, and rot- and rust-free plastic and vinyl pipes that are now commonly used in plumbing systems.

schematic diagram: An illustration of the components of a system that uses abstract, graphic symbols instead of realistic pictures or illustrations.

sewer: A usually underground channel that is used to send water and waste matter to water and sewage treatment plants. The sewer is connected via pipes to plumbing systems in homes, factories, and other structures.

sewer system: A plumbing system that is made up of a sewer and a sewage disposal system.

solder: A metal alloy that is heated to create a permanent bond between metal components.

soldering paste: A type of cement that is applied to a pipe where the pipe joins the fitting to create a bond before the two components are soldered together. Also known as **flux**.

sweating pipe: The process of using a propane torch to heat a pipe and fitting to a temperature in which solder can be applied that will permanently join the two components.

Words to Understand

apprenticeship: A formal training program that combines classroom instruction and supervised practical experience. Apprentices are paid a salary that increases as they obtain experience. A registered apprenticeship program is one that is approved by the U.S. Department of Labor. Similar programs exist in other countries.

community college: A private or public two-year college that awards certificates and associate degrees.

fringe benefits: A payment or non-financial benefit that is given to a worker in addition to salary. These consist of cash bonuses for good work, paid vacations and sick days, and health and life insurance.

technical college: A public or private college that offers two- or four-year programs in practical subjects, such as the trades, information technology, applied sciences, agriculture, and engineering.

union: An organization that seeks to gain better wages, benefits, and working conditions for its members. Also called a **labor union** or **trade union**.

CHAPTER 4

Preparing for the Field and Making a Living

Educational Paths

Interested in becoming a plumber? If so, there are several educational paths that will prepare you to work in this exciting field. Many aspiring plumbers participate in an apprenticeship. Others earn an associate degree in plumbing technology, receive training in the military, participate in training programs offered by contractors, or learn through informal methods such as working as a helper to an experienced plumber. Many people want to enter this career, so you'll need to work hard and not give up during your studies.

High School Classes

Before you begin your training, be sure to take classes and participate in clubs and programs that will make you well-prepared after graduation. Shop classes offer a great

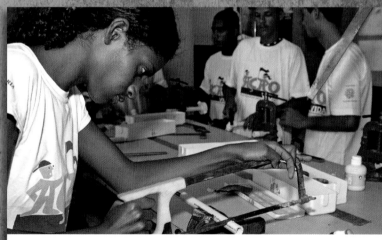

■ *Teenagers in Brazil learn plumbing skills, including how to use a hacksaw to cut PVC pipe.*

introduction to construction concepts, safety practices, and the use of hand and power tools. Many new plumbing products incorporate wired or wireless technology, so it's also a good idea to take electronics classes.

■ *A teacher discusses plumbing concepts with community college students.*

Mathematics classes are important because plumbers use math throughout their work days. They need basic math skills to determine measurements, create job estimates, manage budgets, prepare invoices, and set payroll (if they own a contracting business). They need more advanced math skills to assess the amount of water pressure running through pipes, to calculate offsets and angles for piping, and assess numerical information on blueprints, building plans, and diagrams.

If you want to start your own contracting business, you'll need to take business, accounting, marketing, English/writing, and computer science classes. Business and accounting courses will help you to manage the financial and managerial aspects of owning a business. Marketing classes will teach you how to advertise your services and connect with customers. English and writing classes will help you to write marketing material and better communicate with customers and your employees. Knowledge of computers and information technology is a must for anyone in our high-tech society. As an apprentice, you might use computers to participate in training simulations or to take tests. On the job, you'll use digital devices for measuring and tablet computers to review blueprints. As a business owner, knowledge of technology and the internet will help you to use computers, apps, and other technology to track customer appointments, maintain records, and perform basic accounting. It will also help you to effectively use the internet and social media to advertise your business and interact with customers and employees.

Some technical high schools offer specialized programs in plumbing. In some programs, you can earn credits toward future completion of an apprenticeship program. Here are some typical tasks and topics you'll learn about in such a program:

- Soldering techniques
- Pipe threading
- Joining pipes with solvent cement
- Water supply and distribution systems
- Sanitary waste and venting systems
- Fixture and appliance installation
- Safety practices
- Troubleshooting strategies
- Blueprint reading and estimating
- National and state building codes

In many programs, students develop their skills by working on a mock house in the shop area. They learn how to install a complete plumbing system that includes plumbing fixtures, a hot water heater, and waste and vent piping. They also learn how to repair and service existing plumbing fixtures.

Pre-Apprenticeships

Some aspiring plumbers participate in pre-apprenticeship programs before entering an apprenticeship program. This allows them to learn about the trades and see if a career as a plumber is a good fit for their skills and interests. These programs are offered by professional associations, **community colleges**, and **unions**. For example, the Plumbing-Heating-Cooling Contractors Association offers a six-week HVAC & Plumbing Pre-Apprenticeship Course, an online program that features the following course modules: Introduction to the Trades, Soft Skills, Basic Math Skills, Tools, Safety, and Introduction to Construction Drawings.

In the United States, Associated Builders and Contractors offers a pre-apprenticeship program that prepares students to enter a registered apprenticeship program. Some of the modules completed by participants include:

- Introduction to Construction Math
- Introduction to Hand Tools

- Introduction to Power Tools
- Introduction to Construction Drawings
- Introduction to Material Handling
- Plumbing Safety
- Pipes and Fittings
- Introduction to Plumbing Fixtures
- Introduction to Drain, Waste, and Vent Systems
- Introduction to Water Distribution Systems

The National Association of Home Builders offers pre-apprenticeship certificate training through the Home Builders Institute. The program is geared toward high school and college students, transitioning military members, veterans, justice-involved youth and adults, and unemployed and displaced workers. Programs are available in plumbing, carpentry, building construction technology, weatherization, electrical, landscaping, masonry, and painting.

■ *Female apprentices and journeymen plumbers and pipefitters discuss the benefits of working in the field, the apprenticeship process, and pre-apprenticeship programs.*

Apprenticeships

The majority of people train to become plumbers by completing an apprenticeship program, which typically lasts four to five years. In the United States, trainees complete a minimum of 2,000 hours of on-the-job training and 144 hours of related classroom instruction during each year of training. Some programs require more hands-on and classroom training.

■ *A plumber provides tips to a plumber helper as he works on a sink repair.*

Apprenticeship programs are offered by regional and district councils of the United Association-Union of Plumbers, Fitters, Welders, and Service Techs; Associated Builders and Contractors (in the U.S. and Canada); and other organizations. Entry requirements vary by program, but typical requirements include:

- Minimum age of eighteen
- High school education
- One year of high school algebra
- Qualifying score on an aptitude test
- No use of illegal drugs

Visit http://www.doleta.gov/OA/sainformation.cfm for information on apprenticeship training programs in the United States. If you live in another country, contact your nation's department of labor to learn more about training programs.

Those who complete a plumber apprenticeship training program are known as *journeymen plumbers*. Plumbers who work as contractors must be licensed in most U.S. states. The requirements vary by state, but many states require that plumbers have a certain level of educational and work experience and pass an examination. Licensing requirements vary in other countries; departments of labor or licensing can provide

Plumber Career Ladder

1. Business Owner
2. Project Superintendent
3. Foreman
4. Journeyman Plumber
5. Apprentice Plumber

more information. After five years (time requirements vary by state, province, and country), a journeyman plumber can apply to the appropriate government agency to become licensed as a master plumber.

Technical and Community College

Many **technical colleges** and community colleges offer certificates and associate degrees in plumbing technology or general construction. Many degree programs are affiliated with unions or contractor organizations. Degree and certificate programs feature a combination of classwork, shop work, and hands-on experience via an internship or informal apprenticeship with a construction firm. Typical classes in a plumbing associate degree program include:

■ *Earning an associate degree in plumbing technology allows you to enter the workforce in two years. Above, college plumbing students train to unclog a washbasin.*

- Basic Rigging
- Electronics Survey
- Introduction to the Plumbing Trades
- Introduction to Plumbing and Drawing
- Introduction to Piping Systems
- Introduction to Plumbing Fixtures
- Plumbing Codes
- Pipe Fitting Tools and Motorized Equipment
- Advanced Blueprint Reading
- Hangers, Supports, and Field Testing
- Special Piping
- Introduction to Control Circuit Troubleshooting
- Hydronic Heating and Cooling Systems
- Energy Management
- Welding Theory & Practical

■ *Get a fast-paced, music-video-like glimpse of a day in the life of a plumbing student.*

Informal Training Opportunities

Another way to learn how to become a plumber is to work for three to five years as a plumber helper at a construction site or for a self-employed plumber. In the beginning, you'll probably just dig ditches, carry tools and supplies back and forth, and clean work areas. Your job duties will expand as you gain experience (and take some plumbing courses at a technical college). Eventually, you'll be asked to cut, thread, and join pipes, and install plumbing fixtures.

Military

Tanks and guns are probably what most people think of when they hear the word "military." But did you know that militaries around the world need plumbers, pipefitters, and steamfitters to build pipe systems for water, steam, gas, and waste? Plus, toilets and sinks can break, piping can freeze or become blocked, or other plumbing projects can emerge—creating a need for plumbers to conduct repairs and regular maintenance. Plumbers, pipefitters, and steamfitters are also needed to build, repair, and maintain hydraulic (fluid pressure) and pneumatic (air pressure) systems on aircraft, missiles, and ships. Four U.S. military branches (Air Force, Army, Marines, Navy), as well as many militaries in other countries, provide training for plumbers. Job training in the U.S. military branches consists of both classroom sessions and hands-on experience. In the military, you'll learn how to install, operate, and repair

■ *Two plumbers check the level of a pipe for a newly installed septic tank at a school.*

Which Educational Path is Best for Me?

All these training options might seem overwhelming. "Which is best?" you might ask yourself. There is no right answer. You should pick the training option that is the best match for your learning style, personality, and employment goals. Here's a breakdown of your options and the pros and cons:

Apprenticeship

Pros: The most popular training path for aspiring plumbers because it provides a clear path to employment. You make money while you work (unlike college), and your pay increases as you gain experience.

Con: Programs last four to five years.

A Good Fit: For those who like a structured environment that combines both classroom and hands-on training.

Technical School/Community College

Pros: Programs are shorter than apprenticeships—typically one to two years.

Cons: You must pay tuition and you do not get paid like apprentices do.

A Good Fit: For those who want to enter the workforce more quickly.

Informal Training

Pros: Allows you to get to work right away and receive a salary.

Cons: Training might not be as detailed as an apprenticeship or degree program.

A Good Fit: For those who do not need a structured educational setting to learn, and who are able to pick up their skills and knowledge on the job.

Military Training

Pros: You receive quality training and a salary.

Cons: You will be required to serve your country for two or more years anyplace in the world, including in a war zone.

A Good Fit: For those who respect authority, can follow instructions, and have a disciplined personality.

■ *Contractors with successful businesses can earn $90,000 to $200,000 or more a year.*

pipe systems; install and repair plumbing fixtures and boiler controls; repair and maintain hydraulic and pneumatic systems; and much more.

There are a few pros and cons to keep in mind if you decide to receive your training through the military. The plusses include full pay and benefits while you train, and you won't have to pay any tuition (as you would if you attended a technical college). The potential drawbacks are: you'll have to make a service commitment of two to four years; you're not guaranteed a job as a plumber if you enlist (you might end up being an infantryperson or driver); and, even if you become a plumber, you could be assigned to work in a war zone.

Other Training Opportunities

Some large contractors have their own training programs. They are not official apprenticeship programs, but they offer similar classroom and on-the-job instruction.

Getting a Job

There are many strategies you can use to get a job once you complete your training. You might get a job offer through your apprenticeship program or through your college's career services office, but, if not, you'll have to look for a job. Here are some popular job-search strategies:

Start Networking. It's estimated that 85 percent of all jobs are filled via networking. Some people think networking involves going up to people you don't know at career fairs and other events or pretending you like someone just to get a job. Neither of these viewpoints is really true, although you will occasionally interact with people you don't know when you network. Networking is just a way to trade information with others who are seeking a job. You tell people you are looking for a job, exchange information about job openings and good employers, and help others who are looking for a job. Your professional network consists of the following types of people:

- Fellow apprentices and classmates

- Instructors

- Job superintendents

- Your family or friends who know people in the construction industry

- People you meet at plumbing industry events

- People you meet online, including at social networking sites such as LinkedIn.

But this list is just a start. You should make it known to everyone you know that you're looking for a job. You never know who can direct you to your next job.

Check Out Job Boards. Plumbing jobs can be discovered by checking out internet job boards that allow users to search by job type, employer name, geographic region, salary, and other criteria. Here are a few popular job boards:

The Benefits of Union Membership

- Higher pay, better benefits, and more job security than those who are not members of unions
- Access to training opportunities and leadership development programs
- Excellent networking opportunities
- Support and representation when you have problems at work (discrimination, unfair labor practices, etc.)
- Cannot be fired without "just cause." This means that there must be a legitimate reason (breaking rules, etc.) to fire you. Many nonunion workers are considered "at-will" employees, which means they can be fired at any time for almost any reason.

- https://www.indeed.com
- https://www.monster.com
- https://www.glassdoor.com
- https://www.linkedin.com
- https://www.usajobs.gov (U.S. federal government job board)
- https://www.jobbank.gc.ca (Canadian federal government job board)

Join and Use the Resources of Unions and Professional Associations.
About 14 percent of all construction workers in the United States belong to a union. The main union for plumbers in the United States and Canada is the United Association (UA)-Union of Plumbers, Fitters, Welders, and Service Techs. In the United Kingdom, plumbers are members of Unite; in Australia, the Plumbing and Pipe Trades Employees Union; and in Ireland, the Technical Engineering and Electrical Union. Many countries have unions for plumbers and other trades professionals.

Professional associations also offer many useful resources such as membership, training opportunities, networking events, and certification. Most countries have at least one professional association for plumbers or construction contractors. For example, major organizations in the United States include Associated General Contractors of America, Home Builders Institute, Mechanical Contractors Association of America, National Association of Home Builders, and the Plumbing-Heating-Cooling Contractors Association. The Association of Plumbing & Heating Contractors is a trade association for plumbers and heating professionals in England and Wales. The Master Plumbers and Mechanical Services Association of Australia is the largest plumbing industry association in that country.

How Much Can I Earn?

The occupation of plumber is one of the highest-paying trade careers. Earnings will put you solidly in the middle class (a category that is based on what a person earns—typically 25 percent to 65 percent of household income) in many countries. That's pretty cool for a career that doesn't require an expensive four-year degree.

Another cool thing: if you choose to train via an apprenticeship, you'll receive a salary that increases as you learn and obtain experience. This is an important point because the cost of college education has risen very fast in the United States and other countries. The average U.S. college undergraduate has $37,172 in student loan debt, according to The Institute for College Access & Success. As an apprentice, you'll start out by earning between 30 percent and 50 percent of what journeymen plumbers make. The U.S. Department of Labor (USDL) reports that the average starting salary for apprentices is $60,000.

You can also prepare for the field by working as a plumber helper. They earn median salaries of $29,030, according to the USDL. Earnings for helpers range from less than $20,570 to $43,470 or more.

■ *Learn about the great salaries for plumbers.*

Average Earnings

Plumbers, pipefitters, and steamfitters are amongst the highest-paid trades workers. They earn average annual salaries of $56,030, according to the USDL. This is much higher than the average pay ($47,580) for all construction trades workers. Ten percent of plumbers (typically those without much experience) earn $30,430 a year.

The USDL reports the following average yearly earnings for plumbers, pipefitters, and steamfitters by type of employer:

- Natural gas distribution, $65,210;
- Nonresidential building construction, $58,580;
- Pipeline transportation of natural gas, $58,290;
- Building equipment contractors, $56,380;
- Local government agencies, $54,890;

Salaries for Plumbers, Pipefitters, and Steamfitters by U.S. State

Earnings for plumbers, pipefitters, and steamfitters vary widely by state based on demand and other factors. Here are the five states where employers pay the highest average salary and the states in which employers pay the lowest salaries.

Highest Average Salaries:

1. New York: $76,750
2. Illinois: $75,530
3. Oregon: $73,960
4. Alaska: $71,030
5. New Jersey: $69,360

Lowest Average Salaries:

1. Arkansas: $38,570
2. Florida: $40,690
3. Alabama: $41,460
4. South Dakota: $42,350
5. North Carolina: $42,530

Source: U.S. Department of Labor

- Utility system construction, $52,260;
- Ship and boat building, $49,890.

Top Earners

The top 10 percent of plumbers, pipefitters, and steamfitters make $90,530 or more—a pretty good salary for those without a college degree. You'll be paid at this level if you are very talented at your job, manage other plumbers and apprentices, or live in a big city or other area where there is a shortage of plumbers.

Owners of plumbing contracting firms can make $90,000 to $200,000 or more, depending on the size of their companies.

Members of unions receive **fringe benefits** such as medical insurance, a pension, and other benefits. If you own your firm, you'll have to provide your own benefits.

Text-Dependent Questions

1. What high school classes should you take to prepare to become a plumber?

2. What are the pros and cons of training to become a plumber in the military?

3. How much can a plumber earn?

Research Project

Talk to plumbers who trained for the field in different ways (apprenticeship, college, plumber helper, military). Ask them the following questions: How long did the training take, and what did it involve? What did you like and dislike about this type of training? If given the chance, would you train the same way to become a plumber? What advice would you give to a young person regarding training to enter the field? Prepare a report that summarizes the interviews. Try to determine what would be the best training approach for you.

ON THE JOB
Interview with a Professional

Jake Kenz is a plumber in Fargo, North Dakota.

Q. How long have you worked as a plumber? What inspired you to get into this field?

A. I've been out in the field four years. I decided to pursue a career in the trades after working a lot of odd jobs with little to no advancement. Due to being groomed for college, upon graduation, I wanted to try my hand at work. I felt it was good to get a general idea of other jobs, so I worked at wholesale shopping clubs, in the agricultural field, at nursing homes, in hot tub installation, and as a garbage collector. It was as a garbage collector that I fell off the back of the truck onto ice and broke my wrist. The injury required two surgeries and rehab, leaving me on workers' compensation for almost six months. When I was in the hospital I realized that I needed to find a stable job. Plumbing has always fascinated me and it was at that time I decided I would return to school to study plumbing technology.

Q. How did you prepare for this field?

A. The preparation for plumbing was to first take the ACT in order to get a score that would allow entry into the community tech school. The program itself teaches you the necessary basics of plumbing: proper grade slope; how to run drainage, waste, and vent systems; and the local and state plumbing codes. Upon graduation, I decided to pursue the service side of plumbing. The service industry is different than, say, new construction. Whereas in new construction you have to build in accordance with the codes, in service sometimes you can't. A hundred-year-old house is a lot different than something new. Both sides of the field have their advantages and disadvantages. There are slow periods and frantic busy periods. The classes and schooling served as a solid base, and I learn something new on the job every day.

Q. Can you please tell me about a day in your life on the job?

A. One of the most exciting things about the service side of the field is that every day is different. There are some days where we install water heaters, go on to sewer cleaning, and end with a fixture installation. My day depends on the phone-in service calls that were received either earlier that day or prior. There are some days where we go to one of our accounts—a sugar beet factory—and we will spend days, if not weeks, fixing rotted drain lines, corroded water lines, or replacing antiquated plumbing equipment. My day can change in no time as well. Let's say you're putting in a new stool for a customer. But on pulling out the old stool, you see that the floor below it is molded and rotting away and that the floor collar is broken. Suddenly a job that could take an hour, takes two or three.

Q. What surprised you the most when you first became a plumber?

A. There are so many surprising things that happen! Until starting in the field I had no idea there were as many types of toilets, toilet parts, and styles. It was absolutely ridiculous. Now after installing and working on them you understand why, but, at first, it was overwhelming. What also surprised me was all the different materials and ways they used to run plumbing back in the 1950s and 1960s. Every house is different, but the same in certain ways. It's crazy how some of these buildings were built and laid out—all the retrofitting and remodels they've gone through.

Q. What is the most rewarding part of your job?

A. The most rewarding part of my job is solving an issue and seeing your work actually "work." When you've struggled unclogging a stubborn drain, getting it unclogged provides a great sense of accomplishment. When we do remodels and you see a project go from design, tear out, rebuild, and finally finished, seeing the idea come to life is also very gratifying. When you finally have time, after swearing that this job was the worst one, you look at the work that was done and the difficulties you had, you get a real sense of accomplishment.

Q. What kind of personal traits do you think are important for plumbers?

A. Since I work in the service industry, an important trait is being personable. When you go into people's houses, it's their private life, their safe area that you're allowed into. And sometimes they're uneasy with a stranger coming into their home, especially when the plumbing trade is sometimes associated with a negative imagery. Not that there aren't those stereotypical plumbers out there, but I pride myself on the fact that I do not "look" like a plumber. You maintain proper hygiene, wear your work attire, and do not look grungy. I suppose that means you have a sense of self-worth, knowing that you are not necessarily better than other plumbers, but that you present a positive impression. A positive impression translates into a return call, more business, and the establishment of a relationship with the customer. Another trait is knowing when to admit that you don't know what you're doing. By not becoming aware of situations that you're uneasy with, you could end up costing the customer way more by wasting time and resources. You can't be scared easily, but you can't be over-confident in your skill set. Another good trait is the ability to adapt to changes well—changes in job remodels, timeframes, or general scheduling. You have to know that sometimes there isn't a set time you will get off work because you need to finish the project.

Q. What advice would you give to someone who is considering a career as a plumber?

A. The best advice I can give, and that I wish was given to me, is to not be afraid of looking into the plumbing field or any other career path that might contradict what you think is normal. Try different jobs early on when it's easier without other life hassles. Don't be ashamed of your occupation. I was an honor roll student in high school, and had college credits from Advanced Placement classes. But I was afraid of telling my family that maybe a standard four-year college experience wasn't my idea of life. I deal with people who look down on what I do—until they have a plumbing issue and need help. Or you see the unemployment or underemployment with certain college degrees whereas I had a guaranteed job placement right out of tech school. The only way you didn't go right into the job field is if you didn't want to. Career opportunities in the trades are ever evolving. You should not be ashamed that you're installing toilets because eventually you can work your way up to master licensing and make a very respectable and comfortable living.

Words to Understand

payroll: Money paid out by a business or other organization to employees in exchange for work that is completed.

rehab: In the construction industry, to restore or rehabilitate a structure, typically a home.

sanitation: Having access to facilities and systems for the safe disposal of human waste.

scaffold: A temporary raised structure that plumbers and other trades workers use to work at heights that would otherwise be hard to reach.

vulnerable populations: Those who are poor, the elderly, the homeless, and those who have serious medical conditions.

CHAPTER 5

Key Skills and Methods of Exploration

What All Plumbers Need

There are many skills that go into being a successful plumber. Some involve working with your hands, while others focus on using your mind and communication skills to solve problems. Here are the most-important skills for plumbers:

Mechanical skills. You need to know the difference between an adjustable pipe wrench and a faucet valve-seat wrench, when to use copper piping instead of PVC piping, and much more. Plumbers must make dozens of decisions during a project, and your knowledge of tools, supplies, and plumbing techniques will mean the difference between a quality job and a poor one.

■ *Take as many mathematics classes as possible in high school because plumbers use their math skills every day.*

Manual dexterity. You'll need good hand-eye coordination to use hand and power tools and assemble tiny parts and components.

■ *Residential plumbers must have excellent communication and interpersonal skills in order to interact well with customers.*

- **Physical strength and good health.** You'll need to be able to lift heavy piping and kitchen and bathroom fixtures, as well as carry tools and other equipment to and from the job site. You should also be in good physical condition. You'll spend a lot of your work day stooping, bending, reaching, and kneeling—often in tight spaces. You'll also occasionally climb ladders or scaffolds (so good balance is important).

- **Troubleshooting and analytical skills.** One of the important aspects of working as a plumber is to be able to troubleshoot and solve problems. You'll need to use your analytical abilities to determine where a pipe is clogged, perform pressure tests to pinpoint the location of a leak, assess why water pressure is low, and address other challenges.

- **Detail-oriented personality.** You need to be attentive to detail because your work as a plumber affects the health and safety of people. If you fail to solder pipes together correctly, you could have a big flood on your hands. If you set the wrong slope for a sewer pipe, it will clog because the liquids move too fast and leave the solids behind. If you focus on your job and learn to "sweat the details," you'll avoid these issues.

- **Ability to work independently.** You should be able to follow instructions without supervision, work hard, and be a good time manager.

According to Roto-Rooter, some of the weirdest things plumbers have found in pipes include false teeth, snakes, a mop head, a bed spread, a live badger, and mobile phones.

- **Communication and teamwork skills.** If you work for a big company, you'll need to be able to communicate well with other plumbers and those in other trades (such as carpenters and electricians). Modern job sites feature people from many different ethnic, occupational, and educational backgrounds, so you'll need to learn to get along with others and work as part of a team.

- **Customer-service skills.** Many plumbers are good at the technical aspects of their jobs, but don't have the "people skills" necessary to interact well with customers. To ensure that you get repeat business, you need to be polite, courteous, friendly, patient, and able to explain complex plumbing systems in a way that a customer can understand.

- **Business and computer skills.** To have a successful contracting business, you'll need to be good at accounting, marketing (including on social media), servicing customers, estimating cost, bidding on new jobs, managing staff, planning payroll, and scheduling work appointments.

Exploring Plumbing as a Student

It might seem hard for a middle- or high-school student to learn more about plumbing, but there are many ways to explore the field. Here are some tips to learn more:

Take Some Classes. Your middle school or high school is a great first destination to learn more about plumbing and build the overall skills you'll need to work in the trades. Start with shop classes, which will teach you how to use hand and power tools, build and fix things, and follow good safety practices. Some technical high schools offer specialized programs in plumbing. In such a program, you'll learn everything from proper soldering techniques and pipe threading, to troubleshooting strategies and blueprint reading and estimating, to the ins and outs of water supply and distribution systems and sanitary waste and venting systems. Many programs provide hands-on opportunities to build or repair plumbing fixtures and systems in a mock house. Here are some other classes that will come in handy as you prepare for a career in the trades:

- Mathematics
- Physics
- English/writing
- Computer science

If you plan to start your own contracting firm, business, accounting, and marketing classes will be useful.

Join or Start a Construction Club at Your School. There's no such thing as middle school or high school plumbing club, but you can join your school's construction club. This type of club can also serve as a type of pre-apprenticeship in some areas that will be the first step toward a career in the trades. In such a club, you'll get to learn about everything from plumbing and carpentry, to masonry and bricklaying, to electrical and heating and air-conditioning repair. You'll use tools such as saws, hammers, and wrenches. Your faculty advisor can organize presentations by construction workers (including plumbers) or tours of construction sites. Some clubs even help build or repair houses for the elderly or for those whose homes have been damaged or destroyed by natural disasters. No construction club at your school? Then start one with your classmates!

■ *Watch a contestant in a SkillsUSA plumbing competition.*

■ One of the best ways to learn more about plumbing is to get hands-on experience. Above, a teen tries her hand at soldering a pipe.

Participate in a Competition. Competitions are sponsored by schools, local park districts, or regional, national, or international membership organizations for young people who are interested in the trades. Here are two well-known contests that will allow you to test your abilities against your classmates or students from around the country or world, develop your skills, and make new friends:

SkillsUSA (http://www.skillsusa.org) is a national membership organization that serves middle school, high school, and postsecondary students who are interested in pursuing careers in the trades and technical and skilled service occupations. Its SkillsUSA Championships involve competitions in one hundred events. Students first compete locally, with winners advancing to state and national levels. A small number of winners can even advance to compete against young people from more than seventy-five other countries at WorldSkills International, which was recently held in Abu Dhabi, United Arab Emirates, and in Leipzig, Germany. SkillsUSA offers a plumbing competition. According to the SkillsUSA website, contestants in the Plumbing Competition must "rough-in hot and cold-water lines with copper tubing and rough-in sanitary drainage, waste and vent lines with cast iron and PVC plastic for a water closet, a lavatory, a washer box and a floor drain." The water pipes are then pressure tested to assess the quality of work. Plumbers and pipefitters judge the contestants on the basis of quality of workmanship, accuracy of measurements, proper selection and use of tools and supplies, and proper safety procedures. There are also two welding competitions. These will be of interest to pipefitters, who use welding often in their work. SkillsUSA works directly with high schools and colleges, so ask your school counselor or teacher if it is an option for you.

Skills Compétences Canada (http://skillscompetencescanada.com/en/skills-canada-national-competition). This nonprofit organization seeks to encourage Canadian youth to pursue careers in the skilled trades and technology sectors. Its National Competition allows young people to participate in more than forty skilled trade and technology competitions. The following skills and knowledge areas are tested in the Plumbing Competition: mathematical problem solving, proper use of tools, correct pipe assembly techniques, safe work practices, and blueprint and/or specification interpretation. Contestants are asked to assemble various pipe and fitting systems, interpret plumbing codes, use tools effectively, bend copper pipe using mechanical benders, and perform other hands-on activities. Additional competitions include those in steamfitting/pipefitting, welding, other trades, and workplace safety.

In addition to participating in the competitions, student attendees can visit a dedicated "Career Zone" that features exhibitors and participate in Try-A-Trade® and technology activities.

■ *Get hands-on experience by learning how to thaw a frozen pipe.*

■ *Touring a construction site is an excellent way to learn more about plumbing and the construction industry in general.*

Did You Know?

An estimated 2.5 billion people (or 35 percent of the people in the world) lack basic sanitation, according to the Centers for Disease Control and Prevention. Poor or a lack of sanitation systems can result in the growth and transfer of bacteria, viruses, and parasites found in human waste. This waste can contaminate water, soil, and food, and can cause diarrhea (the second biggest killer of children in developing countries), and lead to serious diseases such as cholera (which kills 100,000 people each year).

■ *Get hands-on experience by learning how to install a toilet; have your parents give you a hand.*

Build or Fix Some Plumbing! One of the best ways to learn more about plumbing is to get your hands dirty and fix a clogged drain, connect some pipes, or do some other basic plumbing task. Ask your shop teacher or construction club teacher/mentor to provide project ideas. YouTube is an excellent source of how-to videos. The following books offer good ideas. If any project seems too complicated, ask one of your parents, a teacher, or a shop teacher for help.

• *Ultimate Guide: Plumbing,* by the editors of Creative Homeowner (Creative Homeowner, 2017).

- *Black & Decker: The Complete Guide to Bathrooms,* by the editors of Cool Springs Press (Cool Springs Press, 2015).

- *Home Basics: Plumbing Made Easy: A Step-by-Step Guide for Common Plumbing Projects,* by Ron Hazelton (Betterway Home, 2009).

- **Tour a Construction Site.** Seeing plumbers and other construction professionals at work on a job site is an excellent way to learn more about careers in the trades. On such a tour, you can ask plumbers questions about their job duties, typical challenges they face as they install water and sewer systems, the tools and supplies they use, and other topics. Ask a school counselor, your shop teacher, or construction club teacher/mentor to arrange a tour of a construction site or other place where plumbers work. Professional organizations can also be of help. For example, the Construction Industry Training Board arranges tours of construction sites for young people in England, Scotland, and Wales. In a recent year, it organized 3,000 tours at more than 130 construction sites across the United Kingdom—so there are a lot of opportunities. In the United States, organizations such as Associated Construction Contractors of New Jersey organize tours. Contact construction associations in your area to see what's available. If you can't find a construction site tour, YouTube and the Web in general offer videos of tours of construction sites.

Conduct an Information Interview with or Job Shadow a Plumber. Some people might think an information interview is like a job interview, where you try to get a job. It's not. In an information interview, you just gather information from the plumber and, hopefully, make a new friend/networking contact in the process. Most plumbers like discussing their careers. Many want to encourage young people to enter the field since there are shortages of plumbers all over the world. Here are some questions to ask during the interview:

- Can you tell me about a day in your life on the job?

- What's your work environment like? Do you have to travel for your job?

- What are the hardest tools to use?

- What do you do to keep yourself safe on the job?

- What are the most important personal and professional qualities for people in your career?

■ *Many people in developing countries lack access to clean water. Above, a plumber in Nicaragua connects pipes for a system that will carry clean drinking water from the mountains to a town.*

- What do you like best and least about your career?
- What is the future employment outlook for plumbers? How is the field changing?
- What can I do now to prepare for the field (classes, activities, projects, etc.)?
- What do you think is the best educational path to becoming a plumber?

If you get the chance to job shadow a plumber, you'll follow him or her around for a few hours or an entire day. You can ask questions about their work, watch them as they unclog a pipe or install an overhead sewer system, and check out the tools of the trade and work environment. You might even get a chance to use some basic tools.

Professional associations and unions (such as the United Association-Union of Plumbers, Fitters, Welders, and Service Techs), as well as your shop teacher, construction club teacher-mentor, school counselor, and family or friends who have contacts in the construction industry can help you arrange information interviews or job shadowing experiences.

Watch Home-Improvement Shows. There are countless shows on the internet, television, and cable that show plumbers at work and the big picture of a building being rehabbed or built from scratch. Here are a few to check out:

- *This Old House:* http://www.pbs.org/show/old-house
- *Holmes on Homes:* http://www.hgtv.com/shows/holmes-on-homes
- Many shows on HGTV: http://www.hgtv.com/shows

Volunteer and Learn. We all know that volunteering allows you to help others in need. But many people don't realize it's also a good way to learn more about a specific field (such as the construction industry) and make networking contacts. To do so, consider volunteering with a local or other community group that repairs homes damaged by natural disasters such as tornados, builds or repairs homes for senior citizens, and offers plumbing/general home repair services to others who need assistance. As you volunteer, you'll meet plumbers and other trades professionals who are also volunteering. If you make a good impression, they might even remember you once you graduate from technical school or complete an apprenticeship and are looking for a job.

One great organization is Habitat for Humanity. It operates in nearly 1,400 communities across the U.S. and in more than seventy countries around the world to build affordable housing and repair existing homes for those in need. Through its Youth Programs (https://www.habitat.org/volunteer/near-you/youth-programs), Habitat for Humanity offers volunteer opportunities for those age five to forty. If you're in high school or college, you can start a Habitat chapter at your school.

Once you become an apprentice plumber, you can offer your services to organizations of plumbers and construction workers that try to make the world a better place. For example, Plumbers Without Borders (http://www.plumberswithoutborders.org) is a Seattle, Washington-based nonprofit that helps people around the world who lack safe plumbing and sanitation. Another organization is the Canadian-based Builders Without Borders (https://builderswithoutborders.com). This nonprofit provides project management and construction expertise to help rebuild or construct safer homes, medical and community facilities, and schools for vulnerable populations in need and following natural disasters.

Sources of Additional Exploration

Contact the following organizations for more information on education, careers, and union membership in plumbing, pipefitting, and sprinkler fitting:

American Fire Sprinkler Association
214-349-5965
https://www.firesprinkler.org

Associated General Contractors of America
703-548-3118
info@agc.org
http://www.agc.org

Home Builders Institute
202-371-0600
contacthbi@hbi.org
http://www.hbi.org

Mechanical Contractors Association of America
800-556-3653
help@mcaa.org
https://www.mcaa.org

National Association of Home Builders
800-368-5242
info@nahb.org
https://www.nahb.org

National Fire Sprinkler Association
http://www.nfsa.org

Plumbing Contractors of America
https://www.mcaa.org/pca/resources

Plumbing-Heating-Cooling Contractors Association
800-533-7694
naphcc@naphcc.org
http://www.phccweb.org

United Association-Union of Plumbers, Fitters, Welders, and Service Techs
410-269-2000
http://www.ua.org

Text-Dependent Questions

1. How do plumbers use their communication skills?

2. What are two ways to explore plumbing as a student?

3. What is SkillsUSA and what does it offer to students?

Research Project

Try at least three of the suggestions to explore the field (clubs, contests, volunteering, etc.). Write a report detailing what you learned. What is the best method of exploration, and why?

Words to Understand

Baby Boomer: A person who was born from the early-to-mid 1940s through 1964.

economy: Activities related to production, consumption, and trade of services and goods in a city, state, region, or country.

infrastructure: In relation to the construction industry, the systems of a city, region, or nation such as communication, sewage, water, transportation, bridges, dams, and electric.

3-D printer: A machine that manufactures three-dimensional solid objects from a digital file. A 3-D printer can make anything from tools and toys, to metal machine parts and building fixtures, to stoneware and even food.

white-collar job: A job in which a person works in an office or related setting and does professional, administrative, or managerial work.

CHAPTER 6

The Future of the Plumbing Occupation

The Big Picture

Clean water, the proper disposal of human waste, and—let's be honest, a nice hot shower—are taken for granted in the modern world. And this expectation, as well as the need for top-quality plumbing systems in businesses and factories, ensures that there will always be strong demand for plumbers.

But despite the steady need for plumbers and other trades workers, there's a shortage of skilled professionals in some countries. The recruitment firm Michael Page recently conducted research to determine demand for specific careers by country. It found that there is a shortage of plumbers in Canada, Norway, Germany, Switzerland, Russia, and Australia.

■ *There is a shortage of plumbers in Germany.*

Globally, workers in the skilled trades were cited by employers as the most in-demand career field, according to the human resource consulting firm ManpowerGroup. By continent or region, skilled trades workers topped the most in-demand list in the

■ *There will be strong demand for plumbers to rebuild homes and entire neighborhoods after natural disasters—such as massive fires.*

Americas, Europe, the Middle East, and Africa. They ranked fourth in the Asia-Pacific region.

There are several reasons why there is a shortage of plumbers. First, a large number of **Baby Boomer** plumbers (some estimate that they make up 50 percent of current workers) are expected to retire in the next decade, and young people aren't entering the plumbing trades in big enough numbers to replace them. An increasing number of young people are steering clear of work as a plumber because they prefer to work in **white-collar jobs**, where you don't get your hands dirty. Others have been convinced that a four-year degree is the only path to a good-paying and rewarding career. But if you take a few moments to talk to a plumber, you'll learn that this is not true. Plumbers can earn salaries that match, or even are higher, than those of people in some white-collar professions. These salaries place plumbers firmly in the middle-class and allow for a comfortable life. Additionally, while you'll certainly get your hands dirty on the job, most plumbers find this career rewarding because it allows them to use their problem-solving skills, work with their hands, work in a variety of job settings, and be their own boss (if you work as a contractor).

Employment for plumbers in the United States is also predicted to be good because of worker shortages and other factors. The career of plumber ranks amongst the five toughest craft positions to fill, according to a survey of contractors by Associated General Contractors of America. Employment for plumbers is expected to grow by 12 percent during the next decade, according to the U.S. Department of Labor (USDL). This is faster than the average growth (7 percent) for all careers in the United States. There will be many new jobs for plumbers because of the following factors:

- Many Baby Boomer plumbers are approaching retirement age, and there are currently not enough trainees to fill replacement needs.

- Strong job growth is occurring in the construction industry. Approximately 1.5 million people left the U.S. construction industry during the Great Recession,

■ *There will be strong demand for skilled plumbers in the next decade. Above, a plumber installs new pipes in a renovated bathroom.*

■ *Technology is a big part of training programs for apprentices. Above, a teacher uses an animation program to help illustrate plumbing theory.*

and many did not come back. (The Great Recession was a period of significant economic decline worldwide, beginning in December 2007 and ending in June 2009, in which many banks failed, the real estate sector crashed, trade declined, and many people lost their jobs.) This has created a worker shortage. New homes, shopping centers, businesses, factories, roads, and bridges are being built all over the United States, and there is a strong need for plumbers. Employment for plumbers in the construction industry is expected to grow by nearly 15 percent during the next decade. This is much faster than the average for all careers.

- Oil and gas exploration has increased in the United States and neighboring countries, and plumbers and pipefitters will be needed to install, repair, and maintain pipelines that bring oil or gas to refineries or other sites. Job opportunities for plumbers and pipefitters in the oil and gas extraction sectors are expected to grow faster than the average.

- Natural disasters such as massive wildfires, tornadoes, earthquakes, and hurricanes will create demand for plumbers, pipefitters, sprinkler fitters, and other construction professionals to repair or replace residential, municipal, and industrial plumbing systems.

- Demand is growing for green plumbers—those who are familiar with green construction, also known as green building, techniques that focus on water and energy efficiency, the use of eco-friendly or fewer construction materials (when possible), indoor environmental quality, and the structure's overall effects on its site or the larger community. In fact, *Hardware Retailing* reports that 47 percent of retailers reported that customers had requested green plumbing products. Green plumbers are knowledgeable about energy efficiency standards for plumbing systems, the installation of low-flow toilets and water heaters, rain-water harvesting systems, and solar water heaters and heating systems.

- Demand for sprinkler fitters will increase as states continue to integrate changes to building codes that require use of fire suppression systems.

■ **Learn more about green plumbing and certification from Georgia's first licensed green plumber.**

New Technologies

The plumbing industry may not be the first industry you think of when it comes to new technologies. But this is a misconception. Sure, plumbers still use augers, wrenches,

Women in Plumbing

Women make up about 47 percent of the U.S. workforce, but only 1.5 percent of plumbers. Trade unions, educational programs, construction associations, and others are trying to increase the number of women plumbers. Seventy percent of contractors surveyed by Associated General Contractors of America reported that they are making a special effort to recruit women into the field. Here are the ways in which they're trying to attract more women:

- Working with community and industry groups: 57 percent
- Reaching out to colleges and vocational schools: 57 percent
- Hosting targeted job fairs: 48 percent
- Offering specialized learning and development programs: 43 percent
- Creating mentorship programs: 41 percent

Here are a few organizations that exist to support women in the field of plumbing and the construction industry:

- The Canadian Association of Women in Construction (http://www.cawic. ca) offers membership, a mentoring program, networking events, and a job bank at its website.
- The National Association of Home Builders (http://www.nahb.com) offers a Professional Women in Building group. Members receive *Building Women* magazine, networking opportunities, and the chance to apply for scholarships.
- The National Association of Women in Construction (NAWIC, http//www. nawic.org) offers membership, an annual meeting, and scholarships. It also publishes *The NAWIC IMAGE.*
- The Plumbing-Heating-Cooling Contractors Association (http://www. phccweb.org) offers profiles of women in the plumbing industry at its website.
- The United Association-Union of Plumbers, Fitters, Welders, and Service Techs (http://www.ua.org/women) offers a variety of support programs for its female members and a video of women plumbers.

Additional resources:

- *Plumbing & Mechanical:* Women in Plumbing: A rewarding career: https://www.pmmag.com/articles/98070-women-in-plumbing-a-reward-ing-career
- *Plumbing & Mechanical:* Women in Plumbing: Work hard for success: https://www.pmmag.com/articles/97319-women-in-plumbing-work-hard-for-success

and plungers, but they also use video technology to inspect deep into pipe systems, magnetic locators to find buried iron and steel pipes outdoors, laser devices to take measurements, and power tools to get the job done faster. Plumber foremen and job superintendents review blueprints on laptops and tablet computers, and some especially creative plumbers are creating hard-to-find parts by using **3-D printers**. Those who own contracting businesses use office management software such as Microsoft Excel and Word, the internet and social media to attract and communicate with customers and coworkers, and building information modeling software, a computer application that uses a 3-D model-based process to more efficiently plan, design, build, and manage buildings and **infrastructure**.

■ *Learn more about the future of toilets.*

Technology is not just changing the worksite. It is also changing the way plumbers prepare for the field. In many training programs, apprentices must have their own laptops and be comfortable with technology. Some union training centers have computer labs for apprentices to view training simulations.

Finally, plumbers must be aware of growing demand by consumers for new kitchen and bathroom technology. Some of the new products that are being introduced include:

- Touchless toilets and water faucets
- LED lights in toilet bowls (for nighttime ease of use) and LED light rings in bathroom sinks (that glow blue or red to indicate water temperature)

■ Significant efforts are being made to encourage women to pursue careers in plumbing. Above, a female plumbing apprentice troubleshoots piping on a central heating system.

- Wireless technology that allows users to control lighting and water pressure
- New sprinkler systems that adjust the sprinklers accordingly over a certain time period based on weather forecasts
- Greywater recycling systems that re-use water from showers, washing machines, dishwashers, and sinks for non-drinking purposes such as for toilet flushing
- Home water-treatment systems

These advances in technology demonstrate the need for plumbers to continue to upgrade their skills throughout their careers. Many of these new products incorporate wired or wireless technology, so it's also a good idea for plumbers to take electronics classes.

Challenges to Employment Growth

Plumbers will always be in demand because there will always be toilets and sinks to install, pipes to be unclogged, and pipes and sewer systems to be installed. But, several potential developments may limit job growth. For example, if the economy weakens and another recession occurs, homeowners will spend less money on bathroom and kitchen remodeling (but will continue to need plumbers for repair and maintenance issues). There will be less money available for new construction and infrastructure projects that require plumbers.

If oil and gas exploration slows, demand for plumbers, pipefitters, and pipelayers will decline. On the other hand, increases on spending on energy efficiency and alternative energy projects will create new opportunities for these professionals.

One final point to remember: demand is high for plumbers now, but as more people learn about this exciting career, open jobs will be filled and competition for jobs will increase. If this happens, plumbers may have to travel to other states, or even other countries, to find work.

In Closing

Can you see yourself installing plumbing fixtures, unclogging pipes, laying an oil or gas pipeline, or managing the plumbing systems for a large factory? Do you like working with your hands and solving problems? Do you like good pay (top earners in the U.S. make $90,000 or more annually) without a four-year degree? If you answered "yes" to all these questions, then a rewarding career as a plumber could be in your future. I hope that you'll use this book as a starting point to discover even more about a career as a plumber. Talk to plumbers about their careers and shadow them on the job, use the resources of professional organizations and unions, and try your hand at some basic plumbing tasks at home to learn more about the field and build your skills. Good luck on your career exploration!

Did You Know?

- About 412,000 plumbers are employed in the United States. Seventy-three percent work for building equipment contractors, 4 percent are employed in nonresidential building construction, 4 percent work in utility system construction, and 3 percent work for local government agencies.
- Approximately 10 percent of plumbers are self-employed.
- About 9 percent of workers in the construction industry are women.

Source: U.S. Department of Labor

Text-Dependent Questions

1. Can you name three reasons why employment prospects are good for plumbers?

2. What are some of the new types of plumbing products that are being introduced?

3. What are some developments that might slow employment for plumbers?

Research Project

Plumbers are playing an increasingly important role in the alternative energy industry. Conduct some research to learn what roles plumbers play in the solar and hydropower industries. Write a report about your findings and present it to your class.

apprentice: A trainee who is enrolled in a program that prepares them to work as a skilled trades worker. Apprentices must complete 2,000 hours of on-the-job training and 144 hours of related classroom instruction during a four- to five-year course of study. They are paid a salary that increases as they obtain experience.

apprenticeship: A formal training program that often consists of 2,000 hours of on-the-job training and 144 hours of related classroom instruction per year for four to five years.

bid: A formal offer created by a contractor or trades worker that details the work that will be done, the amount the company or individual will charge, and the time frame in which the work will be completed.

blueprints: A reproduction of a technical plan for the construction of a home or other structure. Blueprints are created by licensed architects.

building codes: A series of rules established by local, state, regional, and national governments that ensure safe construction. The National Electrical Code, which was developed by the National Fire Protection Association, is an example of a building code in the United States.

building information modeling software: A computer application that uses a 3D model-based process that helps construction, architecture, and engineering professionals to more efficiently plan, design, build, and manage buildings and infra-structure.

building materials: Any naturally-occurring (clay, rocks, sand, wood, etc.) or human-made substances (steel, cement, etc.) that are used to construct buildings and other structures.

building permit: Written permission from a government entity that allows trades workers to construct, alter, or otherwise work at a construction site.

community college: A private or public two-year college that awards certificates and associate degrees.

general contractor: A licensed individual or company that accepts primary respon-sibility for work done at a construction site or in another setting.

green construction: The planning, design, construction, and operation of structures in an environmentally responsible manner. Green construction stresses energy and water efficiency, the use of eco-friendly construction materials (when possible), indoor environmental quality, and the structure's overall effects on its site or the larger community. Also known as **green building**.

inspection: The process of reviewing/examining ongoing or recently completed construction work to ensure that it has been completed per the applicable building codes. Construction and building inspectors are employed by government agencies and private companies that provide inspection services to potential purchasers of new construction or remodeled buildings.

job foreman: A journeyman (male or female) who manages a group of other journeymen and apprentices on a project.

journeyman: A trades worker who has completed an apprenticeship training. If licensed, he or she can work without direct supervision, but, for large projects, must work under permits issued to a master electrician.

Leadership in Energy and Environmental Design (LEED) certification: A third-party verification that remodeled or newly constructed buildings have met the highest criteria for water efficiency, energy efficiency, the use of eco-friendly materials and building practices, indoor environmental quality, and other criteria. LEED certification is the most popular green building rating system in the world.

master trades worker: A trades professional who has a minimum level of experience (usually at least three to four years as a licensed professional) and who has passed an examination. Master trades workers manage journeymen, trades workers, and apprentices.

prefabricated: The manufacture or fabrication of certain components of a structure (walls, electrical components, etc.) away from the construction site. Prefabricated products are brought to the construction site and joined with existing structures or components.

schematic diagram: An illustration of the components of a system that uses abstract, graphic symbols instead of realistic pictures or illustrations.

self-employment: Working for oneself as a small business owner, rather than for a corporation or other employer. Self-employed people are responsible for generating their own income, and they must provide their own fringe benefits (such as health insurance).

smart home technology: A system of interconnected devices that perform certain actions to save energy, time, and money.

technical college: A public or private college that offers two- or four-year programs in practical subjects, such as the trades, information technology, applied sciences, agriculture, and engineering.

union: An organization that seeks to gain better wages, benefits, and working conditions for its members. Also called a **labor union** or **trade union**.

zoning permit: A document issued by a government body that stipulates that the project in question meets existing zoning rules for a geographic area.

zoning rules: Restrictions established by government bodies as to what type of structure can be built in a certain area. For example, many cities have zoning rules that restrict the construction of factories in residential areas.

Index

Photo Credits

Further Reading & Internet Resources

Blankenbaker, E. Keith. *Modern Plumbing*. 8th ed. Tinley Park, Ill.: Goodheart-Willcox, 2014.

Carter, W. Hodding. *Flushed: How the Plumber Saved Civilization*. New York: Atria Books, 2007.

Editors of Cool Springs Press. *Black & Decker: The Complete Guide to Plumbing*. 6th ed. Minneapolis, Minn.: Cool Springs Press, 2015.

Nardo, Don. *Roman Roads and Aqueducts*. San Diego, Calif: Referencepoint Press, 2014.

Perdew, Laura. *How the Toilet Changed History*. North Mankato, Minn.: ABDO, 2015.

Internet Resources

http://www.careersinconstruction.ca/en/careers/career-finder: This website from BuildForce Canada provides information on job duties, training, and salaries for plumbers. It also features interesting videos depicting apprentices and female plumbers.

https://www.bls.gov/ooh/construction-and-extraction/plumbers-pipefitters-and-steamfitters.htm: This article from the *Occupational Outlook Handbook* provides information on job duties, educational requirements, salaries, and the employment outlook for plumbers, pipefitters, and steamfitters.

http://byf.org/professions: This web program of the National Center for Construction Education and Research offers overviews of more than thirty careers in the trades (including plumbers and pipefitters), videos of trades workers on the job, and much more.

https://nationalcareersservice.direct.gov.uk/job-profiles/plumber: This resource from the United Kingdom's National Careers Service provides information on job duties, educational requirements, key skills, salaries, and the work environment for plumbers.

http://www.bhg.com/home-improvement/plumbing/an-introduction-to-plumbing: This resource from Better Homes & Gardens provides an introduction to plumbing and offers tips on common household plumbing problems—such as fixing a leaky faucet, unclogging a drain, and thawing out frozen water pipes.

About the Author

Andrew Morkes has been a writer and editor for more than 25 years. He is the author of more than 20 books about college-planning and careers, including many titles in this series, the *Vault Career Guide to Social Media*, and *They Teach That in College!?: A Resource Guide to More Than 100 Interesting College Majors*, which was selected as one of the best books of the year by the library journal *Voice of Youth Advocates*. He is also the author and publisher of "The Morkes Report: College and Career Planning Trends" blog.

Video Credits

Chapter 1: Learn more about plumbing career paths (recreation, medical, public water supply safety: http://x-qr.net/1Eb3

A plumber discusses the rewards and challenges of the job: http://x-qr.net/1Gr3

An Australian plumber discusses his career: http://x-qr.net/1FWg

Learn more about the career of pipefitter: http://x-qr.net/1Dei

Chapter 4: Female apprentices and journeymen plumbers and pipefitters discuss the benefits of working in the field, the apprenticeship process, and pre-apprenticeship programs: http://x-qr.net/1Fhk

Get a fast-paced, music-video-like glimpse of a day in the life of a plumbing student: http://x-qr.net/1FSZ

Learn about the great salaries for plumbers: http://x-qr.net/1HFG

Chapter 5: Watch a contestant in a SkillsUSA plumbing competition: http://x-qr.net/1Fy5

Get hands-on experience by learning how to thaw a frozen pipe: http://x-qr.net/1G01

Get hands-on experience by learning how to install a toilet; have your parents give you a hand: http://x-qr.net/1Hgi

Chapter 6: Learn more about green plumbing and certification from Georgia's first licensed green plumber: http://x-qr.net/1GJ5

Learn more about the future of toilets: http://x-qr.net/1GbN